BASKETBALL LEGENDS

Kareem Abdul-Jabbar

Larry Bird

Wilt Chamberlain

Julius Erving

Magic Johnson

Michael Jordan

CHELSEA HOUSE PUBLISHERS

MAGIC JOHNSON

Steven Frank

Introduction by
Chuck Daly

CHELSEA HOUSE PUBLISHERS
New York · Philadelphia

Produced by Daniel Bial Agency
New York, New York.

Picture research by Alan Gottlieb
Cover illustration by Charles Lilly

3 5 7 9 8 6 4

Library of Congress Cataloguing-in-Publication Data

Frank, Steven.
        Magic Johnson / Steven Frank
            p.   cm. -- (Basketball legends)
        Includes bibliographical references and index.
        ISBN 0-7910-2430-X (hard)
        1. Johnson, Earvin, 1959–   --Juvenile literature. 2. Basketball
players--United States--Biography--Juvenile literature.
[1. Johnson, Earvin, 1959–   . 2. Basketball players. 3. Afro-Americans--
Biography.]   I. Title. II. Series.
GV884.J63F73   1994
796.323'092--dc20
[B]

CONTENTS

BECOMING A
BASKETBALL LEGEND

Chuck Daly

What does it take to be a basketball superstar? Two of the three things it takes are easy to spot. Any great athlete must have excellent skills and tremendous dedication. The third quality needed is much harder to define, or even put in words. Others call it leadership or desire to win, but I'm not sure that explains it fully. This third quality relates to the athlete's thinking process, a certain mentality and work ethic. One can coach athletic skills, and while few superstars need outside influence to help keep them dedicated, it is possible for a coach to offer some well-timed words in order to keep that athlete fully motivated. But a coach can do no more than appeal to a player's will to win; how much that player is then capable of ensuring victory is up to his own internal workings.

In recent times, we have been fortunate to have seen some of the best to play the game. Larry Bird, Magic Johnson, and Michael Jordan had all three components of superstardom in full measure. They brought their teams to numerous championships, and made the players around them better. (They also made their coaches look smart.)

I myself coached a player who belongs in that class, Isiah Thomas, who helped lead the Detroit Pistons to consecutive NBA crowns. Isiah is not tall—he's just over six feet—but he could do whatever he wanted with the ball. And what he wanted to do most was lead and win.

All the players I mentioned above and those whom this

series will chronicle are tremendously gifted athletes, but for the most part, you can't play professional basketball at all unless you have excellent skills. And few players get to stay on their team unless they are willing to dedicate themselves to improving their talents even more, learning about their opponents, and finding a way to join with their teammates and win.

It's that third element that separates the good player from the superstar, the memorable players from the legends of the game. Superstars know when to take over the game. If the situation calls for a defensive stop, the superstars stand up and do it. If the situation calls for a key pass, they make it. And if the situation calls for a big shot, they want the ball. They don't want the ball simply because of their own glory or ego. Instead they know—and their teammates know—that they are the ones who can deliver, regardless of the pressure.

The words "legend" and "superstar" are often tossed around without real meaning. Taking a hard look at some of those who truly can be classified as "legends" can provide insight into the things that brought them to that level. All of them developed their legacy over numerous seasons of play, even if certain games will always stand out in the memories of those who saw them. Those games typically featured amazing feats of all-around play. No matter how great the fans thought the superstars were, these players were capable of surprising the fans, their opponents, and occasionally even themselves. The desire to win took over, and with their dedication and athletic skills already in place, they were capable of the most astonishing achievements.

CHUCK DALY, currently the head coach of the New Jersey Nets, guided the Detroit Pistons to two straight NBA championships, in 1989 and 1990. He earned a gold medal as coach of the 1992 U.S. Olympic basketball team—the so-called "Dream Team"—and was inducted into the Pro Basketball Hall of Fame in 1994.

1

MAGIC IN THE SPOTLIGHT

It was a truly magic moment.

That's how people still talk about Game 6 of the 1980 National Basketball Association (NBA) finals. Even though the L.A. Lakers were ahead in the series three games to two, things weren't looking up for them when they arrived in Philadelphia to face the 76ers. The Lakers' backbone, center Kareem Abdul-Jabbar, was not on the plane from L.A. He wasn't even in Philadelphia. He was at home in bed, 3,000 miles away, after spraining his ankle in Game 5.

Jabbar had played brilliantly—even with his bad ankle—scoring 14 of his 40 points in the fourth period, including a three-point play with 33 seconds left to break a 103-103 tie. After such a stunning performance, everybody wondered what the Lakers would do without the man who that year received his *sixth* Most Valuable Player Award. There seemed no way they could possibly win Game 6. All anyone

Magic Johnson was the youngest player ever to win the NBA's Playoff MVP Award.

could do was pray that Jabbar would somehow recover quickly enough to play in Game 7 and save the series.

And then something astounding happened. A 20-year-old point guard, playing in his first championship in his first year in the NBA, stepped in to jump center. His name was Earvin Johnson, Jr., known to most by the nickname he'd received in high school, "Magic."

At center court, the 6'9" guard looked up at the 7'1" Caldwell Jones, who was jumping center for the Sixers, and grinned. He felt utterly confident. Indeed, before the game, Magic had assured the press that a seventh game wouldn't be necessary. And he meant it.

Talking about the Lakers' strategy, Magic commented, "We knew we had to run—all game. We had to run after makes as well as misses. We knew we could not let up. We had to shock them." And shock them they did. Even though Jones won the tip, the Lakers took an early 7-0 lead. Soon the 76ers began to recover their poise, and in the second quarter they started to pull ahead. But the Lakers didn't let up. They managed to leave the half with the game tied, 60-60.

Los Angeles came into the second half like a tornado, scoring the first 14 points and leaving the crowd stunned. By the fourth quarter, the 76ers, led by "Dr. J," Julius Erving, made a final push for the win, four times cutting the Lakers' lead down to just two points. Though he had raced all over the court for virtually the entire game, Magic still scored nine points in the last two and a half minutes. Philadelphia could find no response to the kid who some

Magic was on the court for 47 of the 48 minutes in Game 6 against Philadelphia in the 1980 NBA finals. After the victory, he hugged Lakers teammate Butch Lee.

people thought should still be playing in college. L.A. won, 123-107.

Everyone was awed by the win. Even Erving commented, "It was amazing, just amazing." While the whole team had played hard and played well, Magic was the real star of the game. He scored 42 of the Lakers' 123 points, hitting 7 of 12 shots from the field in the first half, 7 of 11 in the second, and all 14 foul shots he took. With 15 rebounds, 7 assists, 3 steals and 1 blocked shot to his credit, the rookie was voted the Most Valuable Player of the playoffs and basketball's newest, hottest star.

During that memorable game, fans got a close look at one of the qualities that made

Magic one of basketball's greatest players. He did whatever it took to win. "What position did I play?" he said in a *Sports Illustrated* interview. "Well, I played center, a little forward, some guard. I tried to think up a name for it, but the best I came up with was C-F-G Rover." That meant that Johnson had basically played all five positions—center, point guard, shooting guard, small forward, and power forward. He was a one-man team.

Off the court, Magic showed the same confidence and determination. Before the game, he helped ease the enormous pressure and tension the team was feeling. Everybody was predicting that they were lost without Jabbar. Who could possibly fill his shoes? But when the team boarded the plane that would take them to Philadelphia, they found Magic in the seat Kareem usually took. As the players boarded, he kept saying, "Don't worry, the Big Fella's here." The players laughed at Johnson's good humor.

Magic was doing more than making a joke; he was assuring his fellow teammates that they were going to be all right, that he would do all he could to make up for Jabbar's absence. This would become another one of Magic's contributions to the Lakers. Throughout his career, he acted as the team leader, giving his all to hold them together. On the court, he never tried to steal all the glory but did whatever was best for the team. If the best he could do was to make one of his fellow players look good, he did it without any hesitation. Off the court, his good nature and easygoing humor often eased tensions and kept up morale. He would almost always act as the team's private D.J. during parties and when they were travelling.

Right after the 1980 championship, a TV announcer asked Johnson what he was going to do next. "Win it again next year," Magic replied. "Then win another and another and another. I never get tired of winning."

A lot of winning moments did follow. Magic would go on to play in eight more NBA championships. Some of his finest moments—among the most exciting in basketball—would be in finals against the Lakers' greatest rival, the Boston Celtics, with Johnson facing off against his toughest adversary and close friend, Larry Bird. During his 12-year career with the Lakers, he would change the way people thought about star players and help make professional basketball one of the most popular sports in America.

During all these highlights, as fans were continually amazed by Magic's showmanship, people would still think back on that 1980 championship game, when a rookie went in for Kareem and single-handedly took command. Everyone knew it was a magical beginning.

Johnson Breaks City Record

Earvin Johnson a six-foot five-inch ninth grader broke the city junior high school individual scoring record with 48 points in the 89-25 crushing of Otto.

Being a very versatile basketball player he scores an average of 24 points a game and has led the team in scoring for most of the regular season games.

He naturally was very happy and overwhelmed when he had been informed that he had broken the city basketball record for individual scoring.

Unfortunately, he was not awarded the game ball for this great achievement "The team and the coach has made the difference in my playing.

In the future Earvin plans to keep on playing ball up through high school college and into the proffesional ranks. He also plans to start a business and to travel.

He will be going to either Sexton or Everett High School so.........
Congratulations and good luck in your future years!

2

BECOMING MAGIC

Earvin Johnson, Jr., was born on August 14, 1959, the middle of seven children. His parents, four sisters, and two brothers shared three bedrooms in a modest, yellow frame house in Lansing, the Michigan state capital. His father, Earvin, Sr., worked the night shift at General Motors, from about 5:00 in the afternoon to 3:00 in the morning, and he also ran his own trash-collecting business. Earvin's mother, in addition to caring for the children, worked as a school custodian. Magic remembers how tired his mother would be at the end of the day. As a child, he promised her he'd become somebody someday and she wouldn't have to work ever again.

Magic's father raised his children to work hard too. If Earvin wanted a new pair of sneakers, he had to go out and earn the money himself. By the age of 10, Earvin had his own business, raking leaves and taking care of lawns in

Johnson's basketball talent was making headlines even while he was still in junior high school.

the neighborhood. Like his brothers and sisters, he also had his fair share of household chores. No matter how good a basketball player he became, he still had to take out the trash.

Although Magic's father worked a lot of hours during the week, on Sunday afternoons they'd sit together and watch the NBA games on television. Magic remembers, "My dad and I had a special bond that continues to this day and there's no question that basketball made us especially close." During the games, his father, who'd played basketball in high school and had a keen understanding of the game, would tell Earvin about the different plays and defensive strategies. When the game was over, Earvin would run over to the Main Street courts and practice the moves he'd just seen. He'd even play one-on-one against his father, who always won. His father would play tough, poking him in the ribs and grabbing him. Earvin would call a foul, but his father wouldn't listen.

The more frustrated Earvin became, the harder he'd play, which was the whole point. Earvin's father taught him how to be aggressive on the court. Earvin also learned how to be a smart player, to use his head as well as his body to outwit other players.

Earvin practiced constantly. "As hard as my father worked on his jobs, I worked on the basketball court," he said. "No matter what else I was doing, I always had a basketball in my hand. If I was running an errand for my mother, I'd dribble on the way to the store. Just to make it interesting, I'd alternate right hand and left, block by block."

If there was a game in town, Earvin would be there. No matter the weather, he'd go down to the courts and play, from morning to night. If there was snow, he'd shovel it away so he could have the court. If there was no one else around, he'd play fantasy games against imaginary opponents, pretending he was Wilt Chamberlain. His mother wouldn't let him play ball in the house, so he made up his own version using rolled up socks for the ball.

In elementary school, Earvin was already bigger than most of the other kids and the best dribbler on his team. Earvin was easily able to dribble up the court and score over and over again.

His teammates' parents got angry, though, because their kids weren't getting a chance to score. Earvin felt badly about this, so he decided to begin passing the ball to his teammates to give them a chance. As a result, Earvin began to sharpen the passing skills that would eventually become his trademark. More importantly, he realized that he was just as happy helping others score as he was scoring himself, as long as his team could still win.

As a kid, Earvin had been a bit chubby, earning him the unkind nickname June Bug. But in seventh grade, he hit 6'0" and lost all his baby fat. By the end of ninth grade, he was 6'5", ready for stronger competition.

Earvin had long dreamed of going to Sexton

Magic's ninth-grade basketball team was undefeated as he led the way scoring, rebounding, and passing. In one game he scored an astonishing 48 points.

High School, an all-black school only five blocks from the Johnson house. In Michigan, a state where basketball is a major part of life, Sexton was known for having one of the top high school teams. Sexton basketball attracted standing-room-only audiences, as everybody in the neighborhood treated the games as the social events of the season.

When Johnson graduated from eighth grade, he was shocked to find out that he wouldn't be going to Sexton but to Everett. Everett was a mostly white school on the other side of town, and Earvin was concerned about not fitting in. Worse, the Everett basketball team, the Vikings, were terrible, the poorest in the high school league.

At the first practice of the season, some of Earvin's concerns proved to be well founded. The older players, perhaps resenting having a star freshman from the other side of town on their team, refused to pass him the ball. Earvin got very upset, but eventually decided to follow the advice of his coach, George Fox, and not let the other players get to him. Instead, he went after all loose balls and started to show his stuff. Eventually, the players got over their hostility toward him. Earvin's ability on the court earned him respect. As Magic said, "There's nothing like winning to help people get along."

Looking back on the experience, Magic realized that high school taught him a lot. Going to Everett, he wrote, "turned out to be one of the

Everett High School coach George Fox congratulates Johnson after he performs a crowd-pleasing play.

best things that ever happened to me. It got me out of my own little world." It also taught him how to communicate with people who were different, a skill which would eventually come in handy when Magic played in college and the pros with players from all over the country.

Earvin was one of the tallest kids on his team. Most coaches would have played him at forward or center, figuring that smaller kids could dribble better, pass more accurately, and run the offense more quickly. But Coach Fox, showing good insight, recognized that Johnson, despite his size, would play best as a guard. Fox saw that Johnson could control his dribble so opponents could not steal it and had a talent to read what was happening on the court and get the ball to the open player.

All the intense practicing and drilling Fox put his team through quickly paid off. Picked to finish last that season, Everett won the first six games, including one against Jackson Parkside, the school that had been picked to finish first.

Johnson calls it one of the best games of his life. He finished with 36 points, 18 rebounds and 16 assists. It was a memorable game for another significant reason. A local sportswriter for the *Lansing State Journal* named Fred Stabley, Jr., thrilled by Johnson's incredible moves, decided that that skinny, young hot shot needed a nickname. But what? Stabley considered "Big E" and "Dr. J," but both those nicknames were already taken. And besides, they just weren't right. The performance Stabley had just seen had been truly amazing. The way that Johnson, despite his height, managed to work the court had been, well, magic.

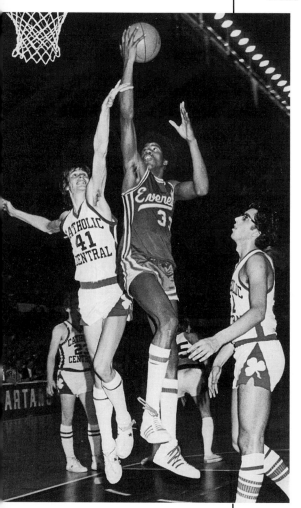

Johnson, already 6′8½″, was named a high-school All-American in 1976. Here he battled in a state semi-finals game against Detroit Catholic Central.

Magic. That was it!

And so at age 15, Earvin Johnson, Jr., was crowned "Magic," and remains so to this day. With the nickname came Johnson's first taste of fame. The more Stabley wrote about the talented first-year player at Everett, the more people looked forward to seeing what the kid nicknamed "Magic" could actually do. Some folks were concerned that the name would be a jinx, that Johnson could never live up to his reputation. It only motivated him to prove them wrong. When he would go into a rival high school's gym and see signs saying things like "No Magic Today," it only made him play even harder.

And so the Vikings, predicted to be one of the worst high school teams in the state, lost only one game in the regular season and made it all the way to the state quarterfinals.

Magic's second season with his high school team proved to be even more exciting. The Vikings beat Sexton High not once but twice. For Magic, those games had personal meaning. He hadn't been allowed to play for Sexton so he vowed, as he remembers, to "show them my stuff." And did he ever! In the second game against Sexton, Magic scored an astonishing 54 points—the most points scored by a high school player in Lansing's history. Another highlight that season was an exhibition game against Detroit Northwestern High. Arriving in Detroit, Magic was conscious of being a "small-town boy" in the big city. The press had written a lot about him, and now the

Detroit crowd was curious to see just how much "magic" this kid had in him. Magic met the challenge head on, winding up with an impressive 35 rebounds and 20 assists.

If Johnson was a big star on the court, off the court things weren't going so well. He spent so much time practicing that his school work suffered. He got mostly C's and D's and his reading level was well below what it should have been. Johnson's teachers cared about him and wanted to make certain he would be eligible for a college education. His guidance counselor called him into a meeting and recommended he go to summer school to catch up.

Johnson was upset by the news. He didn't want to spend his summer in classes, but he knew that for his own good it was necessary. Showing the same discipline he'd learned from his father and the same willingness to work hard he demonstrated on the court, Johnson went to classes for three hours a day all summer and worked at his courses all year until his grades improved dramatically. He even chose to go to summer school the following summer to make certain his grades remained above average.

And then the letters and phone calls from different colleges started flooding in.

3

THE WEAKER TEAM

Magic capped his high school experience by leading his Viking teammates to the 1977 state championship. But even before this, word of his incredible talent had spread, and he was flooded with letters and phone calls from different colleges that wanted Johnson to play for them. Eventually, he narrowed down his many choices to the University of Michigan and Michigan State University.

MSU was located in his home town, and all his friends and neighbors were praying he'd wind up there. More importantly, Michigan State had the weaker team. After his experiences at Everett, Magic realized how satisfying it could be to help turn a losing team around. He realized that he had an opportunity to make a big difference for the team.

Another reason Johnson chose to attend Michigan State was because coach Jud

Johnson's flair drove crowds into frenzies and opponents to despair. Here he is about to pass for an easy two points for Michigan State University against Northwestern University.

Heathcote promised him he could be the starting point guard. It was a position that would enable Magic to take advantage of the intelligence and creativity he'd demonstrated as a high school player.

Johnson arrived on campus to find he was already a celebrity thanks to all the press he'd received in high school. In his first game, feeling the pressure from all the expectations the entire school had for him, Magic did not play as well as usual, missing most of his shots. Still, the Spartans won. And the Spartans won their next few games as Johnson started to show off his magic moves.

From Heathcote, Magic learned an important strategy that the coach called KYP, "Know Your Personnel." As point guard, Magic had to learn what kind of pass each player on the team could handle and assess who, at any given moment, could use the ball to the best advantage. Magic worked with Heathcote to learn each of his teammates' strengths and weaknesses. He also worked to learn about the players on other teams, the men who would be guarding his own teammates. A successful point guard has to be more than just a good player; he has to be a smart player, one who studies before every game. While Magic was in college, he loved working as a D.J. for a popular student disco. Being a point guard, he said in *My Life*, is not that different from being a deejay: "They're both about finding the right mix of control and spontaneity, about picking up the feeling in the room and working with it."

With all the work the team put in, with

Coach Heathcote's drilling, and with the extra advantage of having Magic on the team, the Spartans wound up surprising everybody, winning 25 out of 30 games. Johnson attributes their turnaround, in part, to the chemistry he had with Greg Kelser. One way or another, he'd get the ball to Kelser, who'd do his own magic. Nicknamed Special K, Greg was such a great jumper that people said he had pogo sticks built into his legs. Shooting forward Jay Vincent—once Magic's rival in high school— also added scoring punch.

Off the court, Johnson kept himself in good academic standing. He majored in telecommunications, which would come in handy later in his career when he worked as a color commentator for NBC. He also minored in education. As part of his program, he had to teach a class of fourth-grade students. You can just imagine what all those fourth graders must have felt looking up at the 6′9″ player.

The greatest event in his college career, as he remembers, was meeting a woman named Earleatha Kelly. Magic says he knew within a week that she would be the woman he'd marry. He was right. Kelly, nicknamed "Cookie," not only became his wife but also the mother of his son, Earvin Johnson III.

Before Magic's second season with the Spartans, a reporter from *Sports Illustrated* contacted him. They were working on their annual issue on college basketball, and they wanted Magic on the cover. The cover photograph—a picture of Johnson putting in a layup while wearing a tuxedo, top hat, and tails— changed his life. If he'd been a local celebrity before, he was now a familiar face all over the country. People would stop him on the street and ask for his autograph.

The excitement over the magazine cover was just a hint of what was to come that season. The season got off to a lightning-bolt start, with the Spartans winning the first few games easily and becoming named number one team in the country by the Associated Press. But the winning streak didn't last and the team suffered a string of painful losses, including a particularly humiliating one to Northwestern University, considered the weakest team in the conference. Johnson took the losses particularly hard, as the press began to question what had happened to the magic.

The team met with Coach Heathcote to discuss the problem. Magic spoke for the team, telling the coach that they were being over-coached and needed more freedom to run the fast break to the basket. The coach agreed, and the players made a pledge to push themselves harder during the rest of the season.

Ohio State University was MSU's next opponent. The Buckeyes were one of the best teams in the country, with an 8-0 record in the conference, while the Spartans were stuck at 4-4. The Spartans started out fine, entering the second half ahead by 14. But then Johnson sprained his ankle badly and had to be carried off the court.

In the training room, his leg throbbing in pain, Johnson listened to the progress of the game. The doctor and trainer had told Johnson he should sit out for at least a week but when Ohio pulled ahead with just a few minutes remaining, Johnson insisted on going back in. The crowd went wild as Magic entered the court, limping on his bad leg. Magic says that hearing all the support from his fans, he no longer felt any pain in his leg. Even on his bad ankle, he scored nine points in the last four minutes of the game, and the Spartans won. With the help of Magic's strength and determination, the losing streak was over.

The rest of the season, the Spartans played the game the way they played best, running hard and fast on the offense, and went on to get revenge on all the teams that had beaten them earlier, including Northwestern. By the time they entered the NCAA tournament, the Spartans were playing better than ever.

They easily beat Lamar State College, a small school in Texas, and Louisiana State University. One of the Spartans' biggest bouts was against their bitter rivals, Notre Dame

Larry Bird and Magic Johnson each lifted a second-rank school to greatness with their play. Bird's team came into the 1979 NCAA championship game with a 33-0 record.

Magic takes part in the victor's ceremony of cutting down the net after winning the NCAA championship in 1979.

University, which usually beat Michigan State in football and basketball. During the game, Magic had one of his famous no-look passes, tossing the ball over his head to Mike Berkovich, who shot down the court for a slam dunk. They beat Notre Dame by 12.

After narrowly missing the Final Four the previous season, the Spartans now reached college basketball's top post-season playoffs. They were in the Final Four, facing the University of Pennsylvania, while Indiana State College played DePaul University. Penn attacked aggressively, but missed most of its shots. The Spartans made theirs and won by 34 points.

Johnson was hoping that Indiana State would win its game against DePaul for one reason. He wanted to play against a certain forward named Larry Bird. People had never seen a forward like Bird; dazzling when it came to passing the ball, even more outstanding when it came to shooting, with a brilliant sense of timing and graceful agility, Bird was virtually unstoppable on the court. Just as Johnson had helped turn around the Spartans, Bird was largely responsible for his team's incredible success, carrying his team through an unprecedented winning season.

Coach Heathcote knew that there was only one way to beat Indiana State—contain Bird. To help the team prepare for its confrontation with Bird, he came up with a surprise for them at practice. A day before the game, he told the players that they were going to practice against Larry Bird. Except, of course, it wasn't really Larry Bird—it was Magic. Heathcote instructed

Magic to copy as many of the Bird's moves as he could, and then told the rest of the team to try to cut him off whenever he got the ball.

Johnson recalls having the time of his life at that practice. His teammates were amazed to see him suddenly making impossible shots, hitting the net from 25, even 30 feet away. All along, Magic taunted his teammates, saying, "I'm Larry Bird. Try and stop me." As his team got angrier, they played even harder.

The preparation did the trick. For the big game, the Spartans had one main strategy—wherever Bird went, he found at least two MSU players—and sometimes three or four. They made it as difficult as possible for him to toss the winning shots he normally made, and slowly wore him down. Bird wound up having only 19 points and 2 assists for the entire game, significantly below his season averages.

The Spartans started out strong and remained at that peak level, pulling into the lead with their first shot and never allowing Indiana State to come close. The second half started with them ahead by 10, and they soon brought it up to 16. But Indiana State wasn't ready to give up easily and began to close the gap, narrowing the lead down to six points. Magic made sure Indiana State could come no closer. On the final play of the game, he threw a full-court pass to Kelser who slamdunked it. The Spartans were anointed as the best college team. The final score, 75-64. Or rather, Magic 1, Bird 0.

That fantastic championship game was to be Magic's last in the college ranks. But it was far from the last time he would meet up with Larry Bird.

4

IT'S SHOWTIME

After Johnson's stupendous second year at Michigan State, he knew he was ready to turn pro. The Los Angeles Lakers, thanks to a poor previous season and the simple toss of a coin, got first pick in the college draft. They picked the tall, thin kid with the brilliant smile.

Compared to his small home town, where everybody knew him, Los Angeles was a huge, cold place, and at first Magic felt overwhelmed. He didn't even know his own teammates.

The first time Magic visited the Forum, the enormous white-pillared arena that the Lakers call home, he stared out at the polished, hardwood floor and imagined himself playing on that court. He pictured himself making all kinds of hot shot moves while the crowd went wild. He then entered the locker room, where he found a stall with his name on it. Inside was a Laker uniform with his number on it. He put the uniform on, tears brimming in his eyes.

One of Magic's famous no-look passes. If you were on the court with him—as defender or teammate—you had to be alert every second.

"That was when it really hit me that I had actually made it," he later wrote in his autobiography, *My Life*.

"A lot of people thought I'd never get this far. Not because they didn't support me, but because almost nobody back in Lansing had big dreams. There were times when I, too, had doubts. But here I was, wearing this beautiful uniform. And now, finally, I could begin to give something back to my parents for all they had given me."

In the opening game of the 1979 season, Magic was chosen to be the first Laker on the court for the pre-game warmup. He was supposed to dribble up the court and dunk the ball to make the first basket of the season. Instead, he took the ball, began to move toward the basket—and tripped over his warm-up pants. On national television, in his first professional game, Johnson took a fall worthy of Charlie Chaplin.

Still feeling anxious, Magic played badly during the first quarter. But he was able to turn things around in the latter part of the game. He realized that the best strategy was to get the ball to Kareem Abdul-Jabbar, who could take care of the rest. In the final seconds of the game, the Lakers were behind by one and had time for one more shot. When Kareem caught the ball at the free-throw line and put up his famous skyhook, winning the game, Magic was so excited he jumped up into Kareem's arms and hugged him. That picture found its way into just about every newspaper and magazine the following week around the country.

People had never seen an NBA player with this kind of energy and enthusiasm. During the training camp, his teammates nicknamed him

The Magic Smile.

"Buck" because he'd played with such verve, chasing after each and every loose ball, that he looked like a running, young buck.

The NBA had showcased many talented athletes whose drive to excel and win had captured the hearts of fans. But never before had it known a top-flight player whose zeal and joy for life were as apparent. Magic's enthusiasm may have seemed excessive at first to other players, but he refused to let anyone change him. Instead, he changed everybody else. Little by little, Magic's fire spread, until the entire Lakers team was playing with the same energy and passion. As they warmed up to Magic, the team also developed into a more close-knit unit. Many people believe that the team's closeness, rarely seen on NBA teams, was a factor in their domination of pro basketball during the 1980s.

At the same time, Johnson was constantly improving his game. Practicing and playing along with great players like Kareem Abdul-Jabbar, Jamaal Wilkes, Norm Nixon, and Michael Cooper, Magic learned more about how to play the professional game. "I learned how to get around a pick, how to shade a guy toward his weaker hand, how to get up on a man who shot the jumper well, and how to guard somebody who was quicker than I was." In college, Magic was used to playing a zone, but now he had to defend one-on-one. At 6'9", Magic was taller than all other guards he had to cover. But he still had to learn to counter his opponents' moves and styles.

After showing the league what he could do, Johnson became the first rookie in 11 years to start in an NBA All-Star game. His first minutes of professional basketball might have been a flop (literally), but his final game of the year was a stunning achievement. After winning 60 games that season, the Lakers triumphed in the 1980 NBA championship series against the Philadelphia 76ers. That marked the first championship win for the Lakers since 1972, the only other time they'd won the title since moving to Los Angeles from Minneapolis in 1960. The last game of the 1980 finals was also when Johnson shocked the world by filling in for Kareem and became a national celebrity.

The next two seasons were difficult ones for Magic. Early in the second season, when playing against the Atlanta Hawks, 7'2" center Tom Burleson crashed down on Johnson as the two were going after a loose ball. The doctor told Magic he'd torn cartilage in his knee and needed an operation to fix it. Three weeks in a cast and then several weeks of physical therapy meant that Johnson was forced to sit out until late February, missing 40 games of the season. For Magic, who'd never missed a game before due to an injury, this time out proved devastating. Plagued by self-doubt, Magic was terrified he'd never fully recover.

When he finally came back, he found it hard to fit back into the team flow. The Lakers managed to make it to the playoffs but wound up losing a best-of-three miniseries against the Houston Rockets. Johnson accepted a lot of the blame for the loss, especially for missing a final shot that could have won the last game.

In his third year, Magic was faced with a different problem. The Lakers fired Coach Paul Westhead, and many believed it was because of a disagreement between him and Johnson about how the Lakers should play. Suddenly, Magic, the darling of the press, found himself portrayed as a villain. But all his life, Magic had been taught to stay tough and to endure.

The Lakers named assistant coach Pat Riley to replace Westhead. And Riley's coaching style, along with his team's superstar abilities, helped make the Lakers clearly the best team of the 1980s and arguably the best pro team ever. During the nine seasons Riley was coach, the Lakers made it to the Finals seven times and won four championships. Three championship victories over their archrivals, the Boston Celtics, showed just how far the Lakers had come.

Riley worked the team hard, putting them through grueling practices that made the actual games seem lightweight. He took a style of play known as Showtime begun by Lakers coach Jack McKinney and perfected it. Show-

36

MAGIC JOHNSON

time was an intense mode of play that lit up the court and drove the fans wild. It featured hard drives to the basket, lightning-fast breaks, players testing their ultimate limits. Often Lakers simply ran through the other side's defense. During those fast-break drives, fans would be treated to some of the most unbelievable plays they'd see in the game.

Magic, as point guard, was a large part of Showtime's development and success. His role was to get it all started, looking to pass the ball to whoever was in the best position for scoring. Very often it was Jabbar, who would send the ball soaring through the air in one of his beautiful skyhooks. If no one was open, Magic would take the ball as far as he could go, until he could pass to someone who was open, or take a shot himself. Magic once said, "When we ran the break I was in another world. It was the greatest feeling I've ever known. My eyes would light up and I'd feel crazy down to my knees."

The thrill of Showtime was contagious, and fans started flocking to the games, filling the Forum to the ceiling. Movie stars and celebrities started cheering the team from courtside. The energy and excitement inside the Forum would reach the upper limits.

Magic's winning personality and enthusiasm were a major part of it. He had an uncanny ability to make no-look passes. Keeping his eyes in one direction, he would crisply deliver the ball to a teammate somewhere else on the floor who had a clear shot at the basket. Often the defenders had no idea where the basketball was or how it got there.

During Magic's years on the Lakers, he

forged a special relationship with Jabbar. Johnson had grown up watching Kareem play on television, and when he first arrived in town, he couldn't believe that he'd get the chance to play alongside one of his idols. All rookies are assigned a veteran player to help out, and Johnson was overjoyed to find he was assigned to Kareem. The feeling wasn't mutual. To Kareem, an older, more experienced player, Magic was just a kid, inexperienced, and with lousy taste in loud music to boot.

But there was no question that they worked well together, making one another better players in the process. In time, a solid friendship developed. Magic's ability to get him the ball gave Kareem the opportunity to score thousands of points. Magic is proud to have passed Kareem the ball with which he broke Wilt Chamberlain's all-time scoring record.

When Johnson wanted to improve his shooting, he knew exactly where to go for help. No one had ever asked the Big Guy for this kind of advice, and he was flattered. Working with Kareem, Magic soon developed a hook shot of his own that, out of respect to his teacher, he called his "junior, junior skyhook." By adding this shot to his arsenal, he became an inside-scoring threat as well as a long-range shooter.

While Johnson is proud of all his achievements, the sweetest was most likely when he was first named Most Valuable Player, of the 1986-1987 season, the one considered by many—Johnson included—to be his best.

The Lakers had just come out of a disappointing season, eliminated early in the NBA

Magic's "junior, junior sky-hook" was as undefendable as Kareem Abdul-Jabbar's. This one helped the Lakers defeat the Celtics (and Danny Ainge) in the 1981 NBA Finals. Magic again was named Most Valuable Player in the series.

playoffs by old rival Houston. Over the summer, Coach Riley sent Magic a letter telling him he wanted him to become more of a scoring threat. For seven years, Johnson's role had been to set up the other scorers. But at the same time, he'd been working on his own shooting and had been dying for a chance to show the world what he could do.

Johnson came back after the summer a new player, even more dynamic, even more versatile. Now, he was not only a brilliant guard, miraculously getting the ball to whoever was free, but also a scoring dynamo. He scored 34 against Dallas, 38 against Houston, and a career high against Sacramento—46 points in a single game. His scoring average shot up to around 24 points a game, five points higher than before. At the same time, he increased his assists, rebounds, steals, and blocked shots, and had a streak of four "triple doubles," games in which he reached double figures in points, rebounds, and assists.

It was during Game 4 of the championship series against Boston that year when Johnson hit what he considers the biggest basket of his life. In the fourth quarter, the two teams were neck and neck. They traded baskets, each one pulling that team ahead by one point. With five seconds left, and Boston ahead by one, the Lakers got the ball. Magic was told to go inside to Kareem, if he could get to him, or take the shot himself.

Catching the ball from Cooper, Magic faked the baseline and came across the middle, only to find Kareem tightly guarded. At the same time, he saw that Bird was practically on top of him. There was only one choice left, and in that split second Magic knew exactly what it was—the junior, junior hook shot he'd learned from Kareem.

Magic watched the ball sail over the heads of his opponents and through the basket. "It felt so good to win it," he later wrote, "because finally, after all these years, I had been able to show my best stuff. Now everybody knew what kind of player I was."

5

BOSTON AND
THE BIRD

When Johnson and Bird first met on the court of the Michigan State/Indiana State NCAA title game, it was the most-watched college basketball game of all time. When they moved up to the NBA, they remained the stars of the court, drawing scores of fans to their games. After many years of gradual decline, professional basketball once again became one of the most popular spectator sports around.

The increased excitement was largely due to Magic and Bird. No one had seen anything like them before. They dominated all the games they played in with an incredible intensity and creativity. You knew if you were watching a game with Magic or Bird that you'd see some spectacular hoops.

Over the years, the Boston Celtics had faced Los Angeles seven times in championship

Magic Johnson and Larry Bird first led their college basketball teams to their greatest seasons. Their games together then helped reinvigorate the entire NBA.

series, and the Lakers had never won a single title. When Magic and Bird turned pro, fans could hardly wait for when the Lakers and the Celtics would again meet in another climactic championship matchup. The competition between the two men ignited the traditional rivalry between their two teams, one that had died down during the past 10 years.

Throughout the 1980s, the Boston Celtics and L.A. Lakers dominated the NBA; one or the other played in each of the NBA finals—and three times they faced each other. The old rivalry between the teams was reborn, one that got the players and fans even more riled up about the games. The Celtics-Lakers games became *the* ones to see. Magic said, "No other team would get me fired up the way Boston did in the 1980s. When we played the Celtics, I was as emotionally high as I could possibly be. The basketball was just that good, and so was the competition."

It took five seasons before fans got the climactic head-to-head battle between Magic and Bird in a championship series. In 1984, when it finally happened, the Lakers and Celtics had not met in a championship series for 15 years. The anticipation and hype were unbelievable.

It would be a series that Magic would remember all his life—to his sorrow. After the Lakers easily clinched the first game, winning 115-109, things looked good for them, but that changed toward the end of the second game. Ahead by two in the final seconds of the last quarter, all the Lakers had to do was keep the ball from the Celtics. But when James Worthy made an inbounds pass to Magic, the ball was stolen by Celtics guard Gerald Henderson, who scored a layup to tie the game. Magic took the ball after the basket and looked to inbounds. But Kareem wasn't open, and Magic made a rare although major error; he froze, lost track of the time, and let the clock run out. The Celtics won in overtime, 124-121.

Gerald Henderson's steal and layup led to a stunning defeat of the Lakers in the 1984 Finals.

The Lakers, back on their home turf, sailed through Game 3, showing off their Showtime style, and Johnson set an NBA finals record with 21 assists. But in Game 4, Johnson again made a mistake. With 16 seconds left on the clock and the score tied, all Johnson needed to do was pass the ball to James Worthy or take the ball to the hoop himself to win. But the error with Kareem from Game 2 was fresh in his head, and he became too cautious. When he finally passed the ball, it was knocked away by Celtic Robert Parish. In overtime, the game tied at 123, Johnson was called to the free-throw line, giving him two chances to push the Lakers ahead—and missed both. The Celtics won in overtime 129-125.

That game particularly reflected the differences in playing styles between the two teams. The Lakers were a running team, relying on those brilliant fast breaks that had worked so well in the first game. But the Celtics played a physical game, knocking the other team's players at every opportunity. A prime example of this rough kind of play came in Game 4, when Kevin McHale tackled Laker Kurt Rambis in a blatant, brutal foul that raised hostility between the two teams to dangerous levels. The physical aggression the Lakers had seen in that game took a psychological toll on them. Even though they were all around the more skillful team, they just couldn't match the Celtics' fierceness in the rest of the series.

When the Lakers arrived in Boston for Game 5, they came into an inferno. Boston was boiling over in the midst of a brutal heat wave, and the Garden, unlike the L.A. Forum, didn't have air conditioning. The Celtics fans were equally brutal, harassing the Lakers day and night—even setting off fire alarms in their hotel in the middle of the night. As if the heat wasn't bad enough, Larry Bird was playing at peak performance that night, shooting 15 for 20. With all those forces working against them, the Lakers lost all too easily.

Back in L.A., in a close sixth game, the Lakers did manage to squeak ahead and tie the series. But Game 7 was held in Boston, where the Celtics had a great tradition of winning the most important games. The Celtics fans were so antagonizing that the Lakers needed a police escort to the Garden. Although the Celtics led for most of the game, the Lakers put their all into the fourth quarter, managing to cut the Celtic lead to just three points in the final minutes of the game. That was when Johnson found himself with the ball, and James Worthy clearly open by the basket. This was the wide open opportunity they needed to turn things in their favor.

For years afterward, Johnson would remember the sight of James Worthy standing open under that basket. Because when he prepared to pass the ball to Worthy, it was suddenly knocked from his hands. The Celtics went on to win the seventh game and the title.

For Magic, it was an all-time low. Even though he'd played some good ball during the series, Magic took the losses to heart. Three times during the series, he'd been unable to come through in the fourth quarter when the team was relying on him most. The press even gave him a new nickname, "Tragic" Johnson. Over the summer, replaying those games again and again in his head, Magic became depressed, blaming himself for his mistakes.

Even in the midst of Magic's agony that summer, something amazing happened. He found a new friend, one who would mean a lot to him in the coming years. His name was Larry Bird.

Ever since that NCAA match up in 1979, when it became clear that Bird and Magic were to be the two superstar players of the next decade, everyone began to pit them against one another. Again and again in interviews, Magic would be questioned, "Who do you think is better? You or the Bird?"

People tend to think that when players compete fiercely on the court, they have to be bitter enemies off the court as well. The press and fans began to talk about how much the two players disliked one another. And after a while, Magic had heard it enough from so many people that he started to believe it himself. When he and Bird saw one another at a game, they'd be cold to one another, not saying hello or shaking hands.

In the summer of 1984, after the Lakers had suffered that devastating loss to the Celtics, Magic and Bird were thrown together again to film two television commercials for Converse sneakers. Stuck together for long periods of time, the two found to both their surprises that they liked one another. They had a lot in common. Both had come from small towns and felt very close to their families. They also both knew the burdens of stardom, how the pressure of having everyone's expectations riding on you can sometimes weigh you down. And they both loved basketball.

In his career, Magic was able to formulate close friendships with several of his toughest opponents. The Chicago Bulls' Michael Jordan and Detroit Pistons' Isiah Thomas were both standout players and their teams' major weapons. On numerous occasions, including two championship finals series, Magic had to face these guys on the court, where he considered them formidable opponents. Yet he also proudly considers them two of his best friends.

With these remarkable friendships, Magic helped change how people think about rivalry and competition in the NBA. He showed that it's okay to be competitors and play hard against each other on the court but at the same time to be friends. Instead of hating one's rivals, Magic proved how much better it could be to admire and respect them.

Magic's friendship with Bird made basketball more enjoyable for each of them. They sent one another jokes and gifts back and forth, especially if one was out with an injury. Through the years, Bird unhesitatingly came to Magic's aid. When Magic organized an exhibition game to raise money for the Negro College Fund, one of his main charitable causes, Bird convinced the Celtics to change their rules to let him participate.

If Magic's attitude about Larry Bird had changed during the summer of 1984, his feelings about the Celtics certainly hadn't. He'd had disappointments before in his career and always strove to overcome them. After the painful loss the Lakers had suffered the year before, Magic wanted more than anything else to get another shot at the Celtics. As he later told *Sports Illustrated*, "You wait so long to get back. A whole year, that's the hard part. But that's what makes this game interesting. It's made me stronger. You have to deal with different situations and see if you can come back."

His teammates felt the same way. Hungry for vengeance, the Lakers returned in the fall driven to make their way to the finals. They had a new strategy. They had lost because of their failure to play a physical game, so they would play a more physical game, which they worked on developing in training camp. During the season, their newfound physical playing style added to their already perfected fast breaks proved a deadly combination, and the Lakers plowed through one team after another.

Sure enough, as if fate were controlling things, the Lakers and the Celtics both fought their way to the NBA finals. This was the chance the Lakers had been praying for. They came to Boston with one thing on their minds—revenge. But the Celtics made it quite clear in the first game of the series how hard they were willing to play to defend their title. Remembered as the "Memorial Day Massacre," Game 1 found the Celtics cutting the Lakers to pieces and setting a record for points in a championship game, winning by the preposterous score of 148-114.

The loss shocked the Lakers, but it didn't set them back. They refused to back away from the Celtics' aggressiveness as they had the year before. If anything, this first game loss made them more determined than ever to show what they were made of and ready to push themselves harder for the win. It was time to show Boston the new L.A. Lakers, willing to play tough, to bruise and be bruised. Giving the Celtics a taste of their own medicine, playing a physical game in which they matched blow for blow, the Lakers won Games 2 and 3. After suffering another loss in Game 4, the Lakers, continuing their aggressive play, won Game 5, 120-111.

With a 3-2 lead in the series, they once again arrived at the Boston Garden, the site of their devastating failure last year. At the half, the score was tied, 55-55, and neither team could take and hold the advantage. By that point in the series, though, Boston was getting tired, and the Lakers, still the greatest running team in the NBA, were able to wear them down. Add Kareem's strong shooting—he scored 18 of his 29 points in the second half—and Magic's unwavering leadership, and there was no question who would be the victors. As Magic later said, "We made 'em lose it."

A year previously, the Boston Garden had become a madhouse, as the Celtics fans celebrated their win, screaming insults at the

Lakers. This year, however, the Boston Garden was stunned into silence, as the Lakers whipped the Celtics, 111-100, and took home the NBA title. It marked the first time the Celtics ever lost a championship series on their home court. It was also the first time the Lakers beat the Celtics in an NBA championship. And for Magic, it was a career highlight.

Magic and Bird would meet once more in an NBA finals. It came at the end of the 1986-1987 season, the one that many consider the best season for the Lakers. Los Angeles had become an unbeatable basketball machine, excelling in everything from shooting and rebounding to running and defending.

In Game 4, Magic used the "junior, junior skyhook" to surprise Boston. The basket effectively turned the game around—and even the series as the Celtics could not figure a way to defend against Magic's myriad talents.

The third quarter of Game 6 especially showed the Lakers at their best. Although the Celtics led 56-51 at the half, a 30-12 Laker scoring drive in the third period crushed their chances. Final score: 106-93.

That game also showed off Magic's talents. As *Sports Illustrated* said: "Can the game be played any better than Magic played it in the third period on Sunday?" Game 6 again proved to the world that, in addition to his brilliant passing and defense, Magic was a scoring force to reckon with. Magic scored 12, made 8 assists, and grabbed 4 rebounds. He zipped all over the court and played such good defense that the Celtics were only able to score 12 points in the period, the same number Magic had made single-handedly. Meanwhile, Bird could barely get his hands on the ball, and wound up scoring just 16 points during the entire game. Magic ended the game with 16 points, 19 assists, 8

President Ronald Reagan congratulated the entire Laker team after their 1985 season. Coach Pat Riley, with arms folded, stands in front of Kareem Abdul-Jabbar. Magic is at far right.

rebounds, and 3 steals—and the award for Most Valuable Player of the series.

Three times in the past, Magic had hoped to be named MVP for the season, only to find it going to his friend Larry Bird. But that year, capped by that oh-so-sweet victory over the Celtics, Magic was finally named MVP for the season. And it only felt even better knowing he had won out over a player he respected and admired as much as he did Bird.

As sweet as their victories against the Celtics might have been, the greatest moment of glory for the Lakers came in 1988. Facing off in the finals against the Detroit Pistons, the Lakers made good on a guarantee Coach Riley had made the previous year, winning the championship and becoming the first NBA team in 19 years to win back-to-back championships.

And on April 16, 1991, when the Lakers faced the Dallas Mavericks, Magic broke the legendary Oscar Robertson's record of 9,887 career assists and earned a permanent place in basketball history. He had played selflessly for the Lakers for 10 years, always doing what they asked in order to win. In playing team ball for a decade, he had also satisfied all personal goals as well.

Things were certainly different for the Lakers since the days they'd been unable to win a championship game. And Johnson had come a long way from that young rookie who fell on his face during his first few seconds of professional play. Before his retirement from the game, Johnson would take the Lakers to nine championship finals, including their five championship victories.

6

A NEW POSITION

When Magic first arrived at the L.A. Forum, eager to begin his professional career, he looked out at the empty court and imagined himself making all kinds of spectacular plays while wearing the Laker uniform. His prophecy came true; throughout his professional career, he proved himself the greatest team basketball player ever to hit the NBA.

Eleven years later, on a foggy November afternoon, Magic was once again in the spotlight at the Forum. Only this time, he wasn't in uniform and he wasn't playing ball.

At a special press conference held in Los Angeles, Magic announced that he had tested positive for HIV, the virus that causes AIDS. He admitted that he believed he had gotten the virus after having unprotected sex (without a condom) with a woman who had the disease.

In 1991, Magic Johnson announced that he had tested positive for HIV, the AIDS virus, and that he was retiring from basketball. The following year, he announced his unretirement.

People who are HIV positive usually do not contract AIDS for at least several years and, with the proper medication and diet, can lead normal, healthy lives until their immune systems begin to break down. But concerned for his health, Magic decided to retire from basketball.

America was shocked and devastated by the news. The story was the top news item on all the major networks and appeared in newspapers around the world. At sporting events across the country, fans wept during moments of silence reserved especially for Magic. Many thought Magic's moments in the spotlight were over, that he would now drift quietly away.

But they were wrong.

A few nights later, Magic appeared on the "Arsenio Hall Show," laughing, smiling—looking very much like the same old Magic Johnson fans had been watching play pro ball for 12 years. In a *Sports Illustrated* article, he promised his fans, "I'll still be the same happy-go-lucky guy I've always been, not someone you should be afraid of."

It was another beginning for Magic, one in which all the strengths he'd demonstrated in his career—his integrity, willingness to go the distance in order to win, sense of humor, ability to jump up after a setback—would all come in handy. Magic was still a tough player, only now working on a different team, in a new position, acting as a spokesperson and activist for AIDS research and education. With the same determination he'd shown throughout his life, Magic studied up on the disease. He found out that almost 1 million Americans are HIV positive, that some 200,000 have AIDS and that the disease has claimed more than 125,000 lives in the last 10 years. He then set out to use his fame and connections to inform as many other people as possible. As he said in *Sports Illustrated*, "It's my job to help us all understand that the disease is bigger than we think. I hope that because of my experience people will now learn everything they need to know about the virus."

Magic was soon honored with an appointment by President George Bush to serve on the National Commission on AIDS. Magic was always someone who played to win, and he knew that if he wanted to beat the disease, he needed to get the government to fund more research into finding a cure. He decided to accept the position on the Commission, not in name only, but as an actively involved participant. Magic took this new job very seriously. When he later found that the government was ignoring the Commission's recommendations, he resigned.

But Magic's work continued. One of the reasons he had decided to go public with the news about himself in the first place was because he wanted to inform the public about HIV, AIDS, and the dangers of unsafe sex, and he established the Magic Johnson Foundation to help meet these purposes. He also wanted to show the world that people with HIV and AIDS need not be ashamed of themselves, that they deserve to be treated with compassion and dignity.

Magic made it his special mission to educate children and teenagers, especially black and minority teens who have been afflicted with the virus in high numbers. At the press conference, Magic announced, "I will now become a spokesman for the HIV virus. I want people, young people, to realize that they can practice safe sex. Sometimes you're a little naive about it and you think it could never happen to you. You only thought it could happen to other people. It has happened. But I'm going to deal with it. Life is going to go on for me."

Magic with his wife, Cookie.

Back in college, Magic had studied education, and throughout his career he worked closely with America's youth, running basketball camps and clinics, and holding fundraisers for charities like the Negro College Fund. For many young people, he was a role model, even a hero. Now, Magic was able to put all his experience with young people to use. He taped a television show called *A Conversation with Magic Johnson* in which he talked with kids between the ages of eight and 14 about the ways to prevent getting HIV. Having worked with young people so much, Magic was comfortable talking to kids on their own level. Magic also wrote a bestselling book for teenagers called *What You Can Do to Avoid AIDS.*

Magic's main message: the safest sex is not to have sex, but if you're going to have sex, wear a condom.

Through Magic's life, he has never backed away from a challenge. When faced with an obstacle, he only came back even stronger and more determined to win. He kept busy by performing as a color commentator for the NBA and in a Michael Jackson video. He would become a proud father. And he would even get to play basketball again.

Although Magic's work as a spokesman and activist kept him busy, he missed basketball tremendously. Basketball was the main love of his life. He missed the camaraderie of being on a team, the feel of the ball in his hands, the thrill of the game.

He was delighted to find that he had been voted by the fans to play in the 1992 NBA All-Star Game in Orlando, Florida. It wasn't only a chance to play the game he loved; it was a chance to show the world that he was the same Magic Johnson, as good a player as ever.

More importantly, he wanted to show the world that someone with HIV could lead a normal life. What made that All-Star Game so important, he wrote, was that "by being there, I felt that I somehow represented everyone who had HIV or AIDS. I wanted to show the world that people with HIV could still run, jump, and play basketball. And that you couldn't catch the virus from playing against us, hugging us, kissing us, or knocking us down."

Although Karl Malone protested to the press that Magic should not be allowed to play, most of his teammates welcomed him back to the game with open arms. The fans too were thrilled to have Magic back, even for one more game. At the start of the game, when Johnson walked out on the court, he was met with the thunderous applause and deafening cheers of the fans. Suddenly, the entire East team, led by Isiah Thomas, came over.

Surrounded by all the players, including Michael Jordan and Patrick Ewing, Magic felt at home again. As he remembered, "I wonder if any athlete has ever come into a game, any game, feeling so much support, so much love, from so many people."

Although Magic had been working out and training regularly on his own, he was still a bit nervous about playing in a real game again after so many months off. But any doubts he might have had quickly vanished during the game. In the fourth quarter, he showed that he still had the magic. After hitting a pair of three pointers, Magic matched up one-on-one first against Isiah Thomas and then Michael Jordan. He prevented the two super players from scoring.

With 30 seconds left in the game, Magic found himself with the ball. He thought about driving for the basket and trying for a layup, but Isiah Thomas was covering him too closely. He stepped behind the three-point line and launched a shot. SWISH! It's good! Three three pointers in one game! Suddenly Magic was surrounded by the players on both teams, cheering, hugging, and showing their support, love, and respect.

Before his retirement from the Lakers, Johnson had been selected for the "Dream Team" that would represent the United States in basketball in the Summer 1992 Olympics in Barcelona. As Magic told *Sports Illustrated*, "I want to bring back the gold medal. I've accomplished everything in this game—from a team perspective and individually. I've won championships in high school, college and the pros. And I've won every major award there is. But I don't have an Olympic gold medal. I want it. God willing, I'll get it."

With characteristic discipline, Magic put himself on a rigorous workout schedule to insure that he stayed healthy enough to play and didn't lose any of his skills. To get in shape for the Olympics, he lifted weights every day for two hours, then practiced shooting for an hour and a half. In the afternoons, he played a full-court game along with college and NBA players.

The U.S.'s "Dream Team" featured 11 of the best NBA stars, plus one college star. Magic finally got to play alongside the NBA's other star players, such as Patrick Ewing and Charles Barkley, as well as his longtime rivals and friends, Michael Jordan and Larry Bird. At night, in between games, they would stay up, reliving the great moments from their careers.

Other teams had no chance against the Dream Team. But the games still meant a great deal to Magic. He was pleased that the other teams were excited just to have the chance to play against these star players. He was also thrilled to find out how much the fans and other athletes still admired him. During the opening ceremonies, athletes from other teams ran out of place to ask for Magic's autograph.

And so, more than 12 years since Magic's memorable debut in his first NBA finals, Magic once again found himself in the spotlight. This time, he was wearing a different uniform—for the U.S.A. team. This time, people weren't speculating about the career that lay ahead of him but remembering the highlights of the outstanding career that was now behind him.

But standing under the American flag, listening to *The Star Spangled Banner*, wearing

Even with all his great teammates, the crowds at the 1992 Olympics clearly voted Magic their favorite member of the "Dream Team."

that gold medal that meant so much to him, Magic's thoughts were on the sport he loved. He said a short prayer, thanking God for the chance to play basketball one more time.

STATISTICS

EARVIN JOHNSON, JR (Magic)
(LA Lakers)

SEASON	G	MIN	FGA	FGM	PCT	FTA	FTM	PCT	RBD	AST	PTS	AVG
1979-80	77	2795	949	503	.530	462	374	.810	596	563	1387	18.0
1980-81	37	1371	587	312	.532	225	171	.760	320	317	798	21.6
1981-82	78	2991	1036	556	.537	433	329	.760	751	743	1447	18.6
1982-83	79	2907	933	511	.548	380	304	.800	683	**829**	1326	16.8
1983-84	67	2567	780	441	.565	358	290	.810	491	**875**	1178	17.6
1984-85	77	2781	899	504	.561	464	391	.843	476	968	1406	18.3
1985-86	72	2578	918	483	.526	434	378	.871	426	**907**	1354	18.8
1986-87	80	2904	1308	683	.522	631	535	.848	504	**977**	1909	23.9
1987-88	72	2637	996	490	.492	489	417	.853	449	858	1408	19.6
1988-89	77	2886	1137	579	.509	563	513	**.911**	607	988	1730	22.5
1989-90	79	2937	1138	546	.480	637	567	.890	522	907	1765	22.3
1990-91	79	2933	976	466	.477	573	519	.906	551	989	1531	19.4
Totals	874	32287	11657	6074	.521	5649	4788	.848	6376	**9921**	17239	19.7
Playoff Totals	186	7403	2513	1276	.508	1241	1040	.838	1431	2320	3640	19.6
All-Star Totals	11	331	131	64	.489	42	38	.905	57	127	176	16.0

G	games
MIN	minutes
FGA	field goals attempted
FGM	field goals made
PCT	percent
FTA	free throws attempted
FTM	free throws made
RBD	rebounds
AST	assists
PTS	points
AVG	scoring average

bold indicates league-leading figures

MAGIC JOHNSON
A CHRONOLOGY

1959   Earvin Johnson, Jr., is born on August 14 in Lansing, Michigan.

1974   Johnson begins playing basketball for the Everett High School Vikings. Sportswriter Fred Stabley, Jr., nicknames him "Magic."

1977   The Everett Vikings win the State Championship. Magic decides to attend Michigan State University.

1979   The Spartans win the NCAA championship, defeating Indiana State in what many consider to be the greatest college game ever played. Magic faces Larry Bird for the first time. Magic is drafted by the Los Angeles Lakers.

1980   Magic becomes the first rookie in 11 years to start in an NBA All-Star Game. The Lakers beat the Philadelphia 76ers in the NBA championship series; Magic is voted Playoff MVP.

1984   For the first time in 15 years, the Lakers face archrivals the Boston Celtics in an NBA championship series but lose. It is the first time that Magic and Larry Bird face off in a championship in their professional careers.

1985   The Lakers avenge their loss the previous year and, once again facing the Celtics, win the NBA championship.

1987   The last time Magic and Larry Bird face off in an NBA championship. The Lakers win the series, during which Magic makes his most memorable shot. Magic wins the NBA MVP award for the first time.

1988   The Lakers become the first team in 19 years to win back-to-back NBA championships when they beat the Detroit Pistons.

1991   Magic breaks Oscar Robertson's record for career assists. Magic marries college sweetheart, Earleatha "Cookie" Kelly. At a press conference at the L.A. Forum, Magic announces he has tested HIV positive and will retire from professional basketball.

1992   Earvin Johnson III is born. Magic plays for the USA "Dream Team" in the Barcelona Olympics and takes home a gold medal.

1993   Magic comes out of retirement and begins the season with the Lakers, but a month later he retires from the NBA for good.

1994   Magic coaches the Los Angeles Lakers for the last 16 games of the season.

SUGGESTIONS FOR FURTHER READING

Johnson, Earvin. *What You Can Do To Avoid AIDS.* New York, Times Books, 1992.

—— and Richard Levin. *Magic.* New York: Penguin, 1983.

—— with William Novak. *My Life.* New York: Fawcett, 1992.

—— and Roy S. Johnson. *Magic's Touch.* New York: Addison-Wesley, 1989.

Pascarelli, Peter F. *The Courage of Magic Johnson* . New York: Bantam, 1991.

ABOUT THE AUTHOR

A professional writer, Steven Frank is the author of *A+ Term Papers* and *Sample Business Letters and Memos*, as well as numerous articles. He currently teaches writing at New York University, where he received his M.A. He lives in New York City.

INDEX

PICTURE CREDITS

UPI/Bettmann Newsphotos: pp. 2, 8, 11, 22; Dwight Rich Middle School, courtesy Elaine Flore: pp. 14, 17; courtesy George Fox: pp. 18, 20; Michigan State University, sports information department: pp. 27, 28; The Sporting News: p. 30; AP/Wide World Photos: pp. 33, 38, 40, 43, 49; Ronald Reagan Presidential Library: p. 50; Reuters/Bettmann Archive: pp. 52, 56, 60.